Fun Projects for You and the Kids

by DAVID R. STILES

with illustrations by the author

THE LYONS PRESS

AN IMPRINT OF THE GLOBE PEQUOT PRESS

GUILFORD, CONNECTICUT

TO MY SON
JAIME

The Lyons Press is an imprint of The Globe Pequot Press.

10 9 8 7 6 5 4 3 2 1

Printed in the United States of America

Designed by David Stiles

ISBN 1-59228-193-1

Library of Congress Cataloging-in-Publication Data is available on file.

Disclaimer: David Stiles (the "Author") makes no express or implied representations or warranties, including warranties of performance, merchantability, and fitness for a particular purpose, regarding this information. Your use of this information is at your own risk. You assume full responsibility and risk of loss resulting from the use of this information. The Author will not be responsible for any direct special, indirect, incidental, consequential or punitive damages or any other damages whatsoever.

Note: Every effort has been made to design all the projects in this book to be safe and easy to build; however, it is impossible to predict every situation and the ability of each carpenter who builds them. Therefore, it is advised that the reader seek advice from a competent, on-site expert.

CONTENTS

ABOUT THIS BOOK

THIS book was conceived and designed to give the reader or handyman some ideas on projects for children. It is, therefore, essentially a book on **WHAT** to make rather than HOW to make it. It began several years ago in the form of pencil sketches that I did in my spare time in anticipation of the future, when my son would be old enough to enjoy these things. At that time I was not too old to remember the things I had built when I was a boy, or the things I wished I had made.

This book is intended to be an inspiration to the reader rather than a Bible to copy from. I have purposely omitted all but the most general dimensions and specifications, so that the reader will feel free to change any designs or details to his own liking or to meet his own requirements. Nothing is more frustrating than to follow step-by-step directions from a set of plans, only to find that your lumber yard doesn't carry this particular size wood or that dimension is too large to fit where you want it—and you end up changing the plans anyway. It is rare that any two people will make the same thing in the same way, because of the difference in available materials, tools, or skill. In all of the designs in this book I have attempted to offer at least one possible way in which the particular project could be made, wherever it seemed necessary. This is only a starting point, however, and the reader will probably want to make more detailed plans to meet his own needs. In all cases the projects were designed to be easily made at a minimum cost, using materials found around the house.

Types of finishes are generally left up to individual taste. It is suggested, however, that there should be a minimum of sanding and finishing. Avoid trying to copy "store toys" which are often painted bright, garish colors to make them sell better. It is often best to leave an object in its natural wood color. Flat stains, varnish, or shellac can often enhance and at the same time hide joints that don't quite fit. Remember, some of these projects might become permanent fixtures in your back yard, and you and your neighbors are going to have to live with them for a long time. Be careful of using paint. Paint chips, scratches, and always requires maintenance after several months of child-wear. The important thing is that the objects exist for the child's pleasure, and surface embellishments do little to achieve this purpose.

AUTHOR'S INTRODUCTION

WHAT has happened to the tree huts, the secret hiding places, the lemonade stands? Have they been forgotten in the wake of television, computers and Palm pilots? What has happened to all those wonderful things we grown-ups played with when we were young? Modern psychology has done much to teach our children to adjust socially and to mature quicker through organized and, all too often, "supervised" play. Children's books are today directed toward informative learning, toys are designed to be "assembled" without stimulation to the imagination, and in school, play has become competitive and overly-organized, restricting a child's creativity and almost putting an end to imaginative playtime. No wonder the young turn toward TV and video games.

What about Mom and Dad—how can they help? Working at an office or high pressured job all day, coming home tired, today's parents tend to spend less time with their children than in the past when life was simpler. This loss of quality, relaxed time, so important for families to share, was my main inspiration for writing this book. As parents, finding time to work on a special project with our kids, getting to know them better, is essential. Building projects together is just one of the ways in which this can be done. This time will be valued and remembered by your children, as they grow older. A father once told me that one of the most memorable moments he had spent with his child, was sitting in a tree, and planning how they would build a treehouse.

Tools

Here are a few basic tools and helpful hints on how to use them.

EXPANSION BIT
FOR LARGE HOLES

CROSSCUT SAW
(SMALLER TEETH)

RIP SAW
(ARGER TEETH)

DON'T!

PLANE INTO THE EDGE TO AVOID SPLITING.

DO

SPLIT →

O TAKE OUT
UBBORN NAILS
LACE BLOCK
NDER HEAD OF
AMMER.

HAND DRILL

BRACE

SQUARE-SHANK SCREWDRIVER, USED IN BRACE, DOES THE JOB EASILY.

HOW TO PUT A SCREW IN

SOFTWOOD   HARDWOOD

1.   —AWL

2.   COUNTERSINK

3.

WRAP YOUR HAND-KERCHIEF AROUND HANDLE FOR BETTER GRIP.

ALWAYS DRILL PILOT HOLES IN HARDWOOD

IF SCREW WON'T GO IN -
TAKE SCREW OUT AND RUB SOAP ON IT AND TRY AGAIN.

MATERIALS

1½"
¾"
1×2

3½"
1½"
2×4

3½"
¾"
1×4

5½"
¾"
1×6

5½"
¾"
2×6

BEFORE YOU BUY

CHECK LUMBER FOR WARPAGE BY LOOKING DOWN THE EDGE OF BOARD.

HARDBOARD (MASONITE) COMES TEMPERED (DARK BROWN) OR UNTEMPERED (LIGHT BROWN) — EXCELLENT FOR OUTDOOR USE.

PLYWOOD COMES IN 4'×8' SHEETS IN ¼", ⅜", ½", ⅝", & ¾" THICKNESSES
USE PRESSURE TREATED WOOD FOR WATER OR OUTDOOR PROJECTS.

TO BEND WOOD SOAK IN HOT WATER FOR A FEW HOURS AND BEND IN PLACE WITH AID OF PEGS AS SHOWN BELOW

SCRAP WOOD

JOINTS

ALWAYS PLAN JOINTS CARE-
FULLY BEFORE STARTING A
PROJECT. BELOW ARE SOME
EXAMPLES OF JOINTS YOU
MIGHT USE.

LAP JOINT
WEAK

RABBET JOINT

CROSS SPINE

DOVE TAIL

STRONG

GLUE

DOWEL

DADO
SLOTS

HARDWOOD
CHEVRON

PLYWOOD
CLEAT

CRISS·CROSS

NOTCHED

CORRUGATED
FASTENER
FOR SOFT
WOOD ONLY

CONER
BLOCK

TWO TYPES OF MORTISE
& TENON JOINTS.

WEDGE

1.

2.

1.

2.

NAILS - SCREWS - BOLTS

NAILS ARE GOOD

NAILS USED IN THE
WRONG APPLICATION
CAN PULL OUT EASILY

BAD
(PARALLEL TO
GRAIN)

GOOD
(RIGHT ANGLES
TO GRAIN)

BAD   GOOD
STAGGER NAILS
TO AVOID SPLITTING

COMMON NAIL

FINISHING NAIL

ROOFING NAIL

FLOORING NAIL

MASONRY NAIL

SCREWS ARE BETTER

FLAT   ROUND   OVAL   LAG

BOLTS ARE BEST

CARRIAGE
BOLT

LAG
SCREW

SHOULDER KEEPS
BOLT FROM TURNING

WING
NUT

MACHINE
BOLTS

HOUSES

HOUSES

THERE is something mysterious and wonderful about the eternal hut for children. Remember the summerhouse or the grape arbor where you played long hours on summer afternoons. A house for a child might be branches of a tree, a secret place under the bushes, a hole in the ground, or a big cardboard box; but a real playhouse is even more exciting. A house might become anything from an imagined miniature household to the most fantastic castle out of a fairy tale book. There is an element of excitement in having a house high in a tree where the owner can spy on imagined invaders, or just retreat from the world for a timeless moment on a summer day. A child's house can be a hundred different things in one day—it can change from a jungle hut to a haunted house, to a fort, to a school, a hospital, and perhaps even to a space ship. It's a good place to put dolls to sleep in, to keep pets from going out of, to hold secret meetings in or, occasionally, even to camp overnight. To a child his or her house becomes an adventure—a secret place, which, most important is all their own, and where grown-ups need permission to enter.

TREE HUT

A TREE HUT DEPENDS
LARGELY ON THE TYPES
OF TREES AVAILABLE.
THIS TREE HUT IS
BUILT ON ONE TREE
THAT HAS AT LEAST TWO
BRANCHES AND THE TRUNK
SUPPORTING THE CORNERS
OF THE HOUSE. THE
OTHER CORNER IS SUPPORT-
ED BY BUILDING UP A
STRUT FROM THE TRUNK.
ALWAYS BEGIN BY BUILD-
ING A STRONG PLATFORM.
SINCE EVERY TREE IS
DIFFERENT, IT IS DIFFICULT
TO DESIGN THE HOUSE FIRST
AND FIND A TREE TO FIT IT. IT
IS BETTER TO FIND THE TREE AND LET
IT SUGGEST THE FORM OF THE HOUSE, AS
YOU WILL SEE IN THE FOLLOWING PAGES.

TRIANGLE TREE HUT

BUILT AROUND
THREE TREES AT
MORE OR LESS
EQUAL DISTANCE
FROM EACH
OTHER.

Platform Tree Hut

PLATFORM IS MADE BY NAIL-
ING 2x6 JOISTS AT RIGHT ANGLES
AROUND TREE. NOTCH OUT WHERE
JOISTS INTERSECT.

IF PLATFORM EXTENDS
MORE THAN 2 FT. ON
EITHER SIDE, ADD BRACES
AS SHOWN BELOW.

2x4
BRACE

Thinkin' Place

HERE'S A TREE HUT
EVEN DAD WILL EN-
JOY. BUILD HIGH UP
IN A TREE WHERE
THERE IS A NICE VIEW.
IT SHOULD BE BIG
ENOUGH FOR ONLY ONE
PERSON AND SHOULD
HAVE A COMFORTABLE
CHAIR.

Quiet

FOUR POSTER

THIS TREE HOUSE IS MADE
FROM STRAIGHT LOGS, CUT
IN THE WOODS, AND DRAGGED
TO THE DESIRED LOCATION. THIS
SAVES TIME IN FINDING THE IDEAL
TREE OR GROUP OF TREES IN WHICH
TO MAKE THE TREE HUT.

HiLL HOUSE
LOOKOUT POST

FILL

COVER FLOOR &
BACK WITH LOGS
TO PERSERVE
DRYNESS

FLOOR

EXCAVATE

CROSS
SECTION

WATER HOUSE

CREOSOTE

NAILS DRIVEN INTO POST BEFORE CONCRETE IS POURED.

4 GAL. CAN

CONCRETE:
3 PARTS ROCK
2 PARTS SAND
1 PART CEMENT

SELECT SIX POLES LONG ENOUGH TO EXTEND SIX TO EIGHT FEET OUT OF THE WATER. REMOVE BARK, CREOSOTE, AND ATTACH FOOTING SHOWN AT LEFT. CARRY EACH POST OUT TO LOCATION BY BOAT, ONE AT A TIME AND DROP IN PLACE. ALLOW POSTS TO SETTLE BEFORE FINISHING REST OF HOUSE

NAIL ON CROSS PIECE IF BOTTOM IS VERY MUDDY.

SEE "JUNGLE HOUSE" FOR IN-FORMATION ON HOW TO THATCH A ROOF.

FOOTINGS

WATER HOUSE (DETAILS) 19

LOG CABIN

IF YOU LIVE IN AN AREA WHERE TALL
STRAIGHT PINE TREES ARE AVAILABLE,
THIS IS THE HOUSE FOR YOU. BE
SURE YOU HAVE ABOUT 30 TREES
AND LOTS OF TIME BEFORE YOU
BEGIN. THIS TYPE OF HOUSE IS
SLOW TO BUILD BECAUSE MOST OF THE
WORK IS DONE BY AXE. USE AS
FEW NAILS AS POSSIBLE AND
AS LITTLE CUT LUMBER AS POSSIBLE.
A HOUSE OF THIS KIND IS A RARITY
THESE DAYS AND BECOMES A REWARD-
ING EXPERIENCE WHEN YOU FINISH.

WOVEN CLAY & TWIGS

2-PLY OAK DOOR

REST FOR DOOR BAR

...LL WITH ...MENT OR CLAY

...ARK ...ABS

FILL HOLES WITH CLAY

INSIDE VIEW

FILL IN WITH ROCKS, BRANCHES, ETC. FOR INSULATION.

BUILD FIRE-PLACE & CHIMNEY FIRST

USE TREE FORKS FOR SUPPORTS

LOG CABIN (DETAILS) 21

GOLD MINE

START ON LEVEL GROUND. CONSTRUCT WOOD STRUCTURE AND THEN PILE ON DIRT & FILL.

MINER'S SHACK

DIRT MOUND ADDED AFTER STRUCTURE IS COMPLETED

SECRET DOOR

CONCRETE SEWER PIPE

RAILROAD TIES

SPOOK HOUSE

BEWARE OF WOLF HOUND

NO TRESPASSING

SECRET LOCK

NAIL PULLS OUT TO UNLOCK

STAIRS

CELLAR ENTRANCE

SECRET DOOR

TRAP DOOR

SECRET CLOSET

PLAN

BUTLERS ENTRANCE

5

8

SHOE HOUSE

CUT-AWAY-
VIEW

SHOE
HOUSE

3" LAYER SCRATCH
COAT (PLASTER &
SAND.)

2X4 STUDS

2X3 FRAME

WIRE SCREEN

HANSEL AND GRETEL HOUSE

THE HANSEL & GRETEL HOUSE, MADE OF ½" PLYWOOD,
MAY TAKE AS LITTLE AS THREE OR FOUR EVENINGS
TO MAKE. WE RECOMMEND THAT YOU USE A GOOD,
HEAVY-DUTY, ELECTRIC SABER SAW - A GOOD INVEST-
MENT IN ANY CASE FOR ALL YOUR CUTS. SHINGLES ARE
MADE FROM ¼" PLYWOOD NAILED OVER ANOTHER ¼" SHEET
THAT HAS BEEN NAILED TO THE CONTOUR OF ROOF USE
YOUR IMAGINATION FOR THE CANDY DECORATION. IF THE
HOUSE IS TO BE KEPT INDOORS YOU CAN USE REAL CANDY
AS WE DID. SOME OTHER SUGGESTIONS CAN BE FOUND
ON THE FOLLOWING PAGE.

EXPLODED VIEW

USE 1" SIDING NAILS

$\frac{1}{2}$" PLYWOOD

CUT TO SHAPE OF ROOF

DORMER

PEEP-HOLE WITH SLIDE

1X2 BASE

CLAY

CHIMNEY

1×3

$\frac{1}{2}$" PLY

PAPIER MACHE

CUT CLAY COOKIES OUT WITH COOKIE CUTTER · LET HARDEN·PAINT WITH ENAMEL.

COOKIES

a

1. START BY CUTTING LINE "a".
2. REMOVE SAW AND SCREW ON HINGES.
3. FINISH CUT AROUND OUTLINE.

EASY METHOD FOR CUTTING WINDOWS & DOORS

NAIL SEVERAL PIECES OF $\frac{1}{8}$" MASONITE TOGETHER AND CUT OUT ALL AT THE SAME TIME.

GINGERBREAD MEN

CLUB HOUSE

MADE FROM SCRAP LUMBER.

PITCH ROOF BACK 5'

CLUB 13

6'

TAR PAPER

5'

SCREEN

2X4 POST CREOSOTE & SINK IN GROUND.

BOX CONSTRUCTION

SINCE THIS HOUSE IS SMALL YOU CAN BUILD IT THE SAME WAY AS YOU WOULD A BOX. LET THE WALLS ACT AS STRUCTURAL MEMBERS AND USE A MINIMUM OF FRAMING.

INDIAN TEPEE

OR PEGS

SLIT

Fig 1.
DOOR PEGS

CANVAS

ROPE

Fig 2.

START WITH 3
MAIN RIDGE-
POLES.

SMOKE FLAPS

POCKET

1

3

2

FRONT

BACK

BEGIN BY CUTTING 3 12-FT. POLES AND TIE THE ENDS TOGETHER. SPREAD LEGS AND STAND ON DESIRED LOCATION. LAY 5 MORE POLES AGAINST THE FIRST 3. FIT 2, 15-FT. POLES INTO SMOKE FLAPS AT REAR OF TENT AND CARRY TENT OVER TO LOCATION. LAY TENT ON POLES AND SECURE WITH PEGS (FIGS 1 & 2.)

TENT IS MADE FROM 4 PIECES OF CANVAS SEWN TOGETHER WITH STRING. MAKE 1"≠1' PAPER MODEL TO FIND CONTOUR FOR DESIRED PROPORTION.

SEW ROPE IN BOTTOM FOR ADDED STRENGTH. (FIG. 2.)

JUNGLE HOUSE

SMALL SAPLINGS

APPROX 1"

OVERLAP LAYERS OF STRAW STARTING FRONT BOTTOM

TIE STRAW IN NEAT BUNDLES AFTER CUTTING

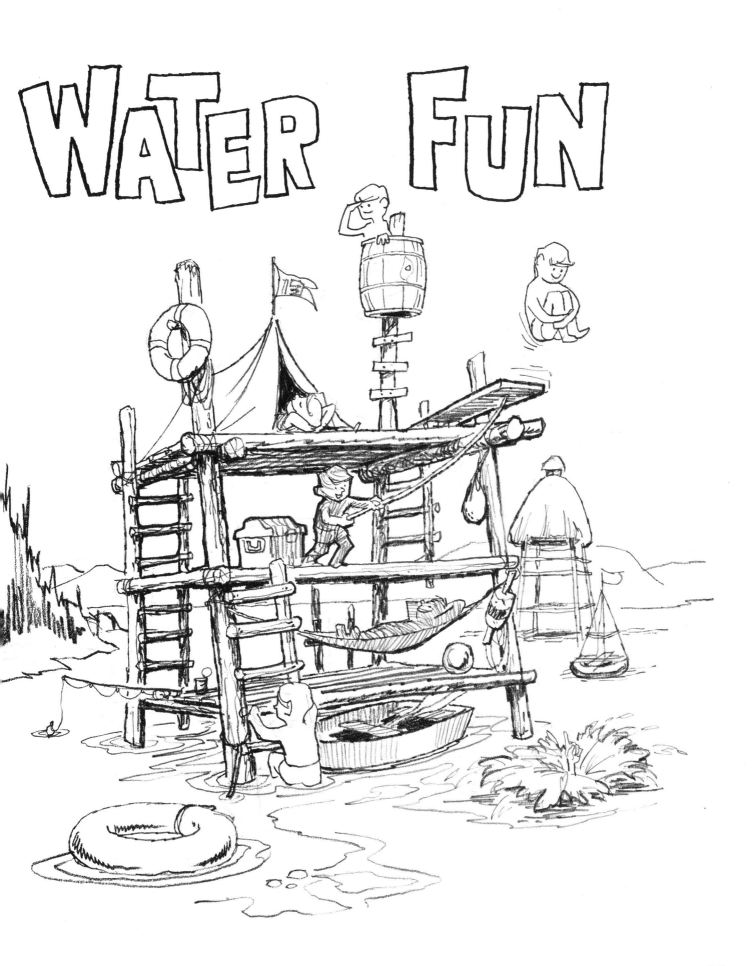

WATER FUN

WATER is the most important and probably one of the most fascinating elements of nature. In fact, down through history man has been constantly trying new ways to use water for his own benefit. In this section are only a few of the possible ways in which water can be used for having fun. It is up to you to discover more interesting projects; your imagination is your only limit. Consider for example these possibilities for water projects: underwater exploration; water harnessed as power; water used to move objects; floating objects on water, or projects on ice. You be the inventor!

Maybe some of the ideas on the following pages will stimulate your imagination. Remember, whatever you build must be safe, and in some cases it might be wise to have an adult supervise these water activities.

BOUNCING BUOY

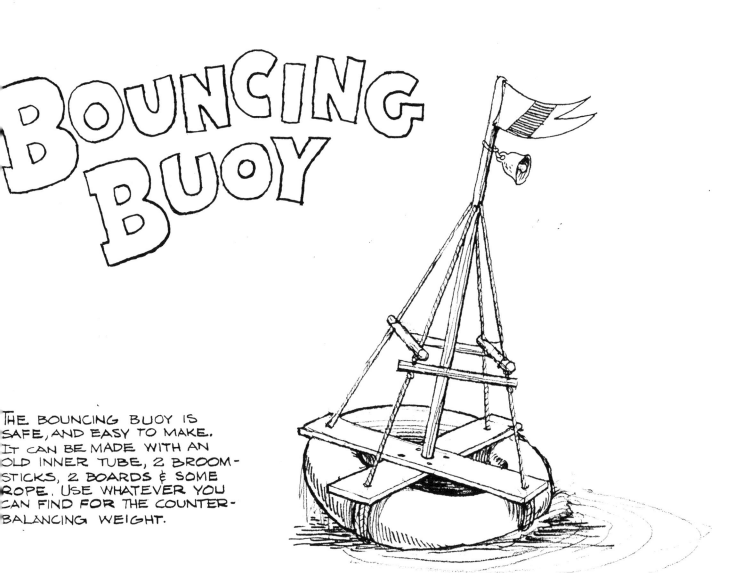

THE BOUNCING BUOY IS
SAFE, AND EASY TO MAKE.
IT CAN BE MADE WITH AN
OLD INNER TUBE, 2 BROOM-
STICKS, 2 BOARDS & SOME
ROPE. USE WHATEVER YOU
CAN FIND FOR THE COUNTER-
BALANCING WEIGHT.

BRASS SCREWS

LOOP ROPE
AROUND TUBE.

TO
WEIGHT

MAST

WEIGHT COUNTER-
BALANCE WITH
ROCKS IN PAIL.

BELL

CROSS SECTION
OF BUOY

JOUSTING LOG

THE JOUSTING LOG IS A SAFE SPORT FOR ANY WATER-FRONT.

THE OBJECT IS TO BALANCE YOURSELF ON THE LOG AND PUSH YOUR OPPONENT OFF WITHOUT FALLING OFF YOURSELF.

BROOM STICK STAVES. WRAP COTTON AND CLOTH STRIPS AROUND ENDS OR USE BOXING GLOVES.

STRIP BARK OFF LOG AND SAND OFF ROUGH SURFACES.

FLOAT LOG WITH LARGE INNER TUBE OR OLD OIL BARREL.

TARZAN SWING

FIND A TREE THAT HAS A STRONG LIMB STRETCHING OUT OVER THE WATER. THROW A WEIGHTED ROPE, WITH A LOOP TIED INTO THE END OF THE ROPE, OVER THE BRANCH. PLACE THE OTHER END OF THE THROUGH THE LOOP AND PULL THE ROPE UP TIGHT ONTO THE BRANCH. TIE SOME KNOTS INTO THE LOOSE END OF THE ROPE TO HAVE SOMETHING TO HOLD ONTO. IF NECESSARY BUILD AN ELEVATED LAUNCHING PLATFORM SET BACK FROM THE SHORELINE.

3/4" NYLON ROPE

LOOP

PULL DOWN TO TIGHTEN

LAUNCHING PLATFORM

BALLOON RAFT

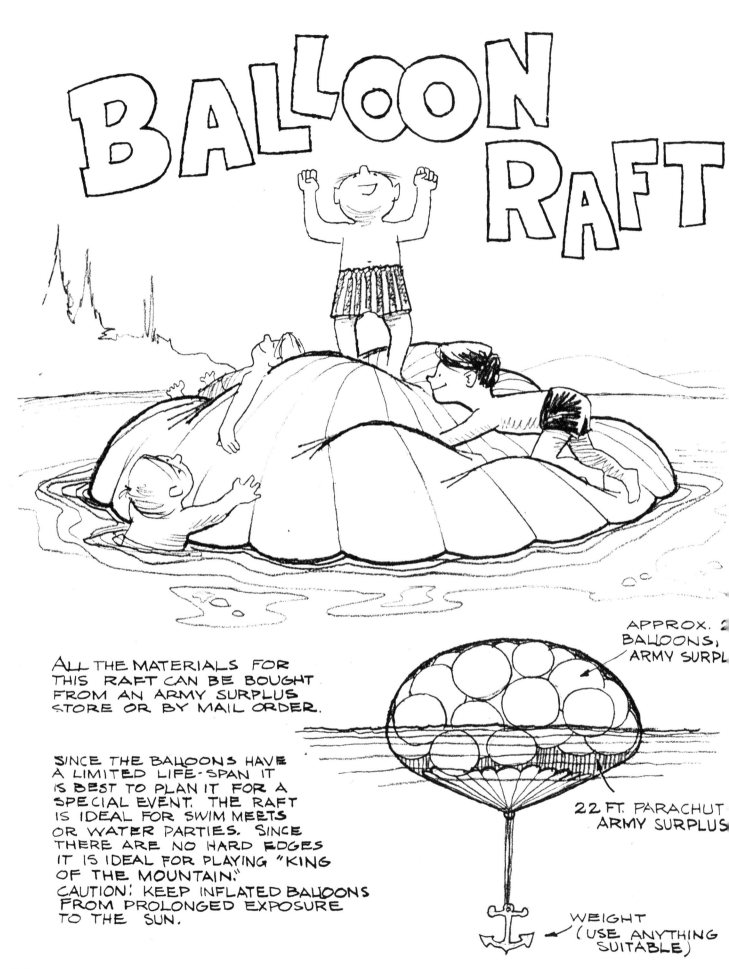

ALL THE MATERIALS FOR THIS RAFT CAN BE BOUGHT FROM AN ARMY SURPLUS STORE OR BY MAIL ORDER.

SINCE THE BALLOONS HAVE A LIMITED LIFE-SPAN IT IS BEST TO PLAN IT FOR A SPECIAL EVENT. THE RAFT IS IDEAL FOR SWIM MEETS OR WATER PARTIES. SINCE THERE ARE NO HARD EDGES IT IS IDEAL FOR PLAYING "KING OF THE MOUNTAIN." CAUTION: KEEP INFLATED BALLOONS FROM PROLONGED EXPOSURE TO THE SUN.

APPROX. 2 BALLOONS, ARMY SURPL

22 FT. PARACHUT ARMY SURPLUS

WEIGHT (USE ANYTHING SUITABLE)

LOG RAFT

CUT FOUR PINE LOGS 10" TO 12" IN DIAMETER AND LASH THEM TOGETHER WITH HEMP ROPE. DRIVE TWO OAK PEGS INTO THE TWO CENTER LOGS IN THE STERN AND USE THESE TO REST THE OAR IN. USE THE OAR AS A RUDDER WHEN THE SAIL IS UP OR USE IT TO "SKULL" WITH IF THE SAIL IS DOWN. USE A BLANKET OR SHEET AS A SAIL.

WHALE RAFT

TEETH MADE FROM PIECES OF SCRAP FOAM RUBBER OR CUT OUT FROM A LONG STRIP OF CLOTH

MOUTH MOVES UP AND DOWN

ANCHOR SECURELY.

A <u>WHALE RAFT</u> CAN BE A LOT OF FUN FOR CHILDREN AND AT THE SAME TIME SERVE AS A SAFETY FEATURE AT SWIMMING AREAS. THE MOUTH OF THE WHALE OPENS AND CLOSES BY PULLING A ROPE ATTACHED TO THE FRONT UP AND RUNNING THROUGH A PULLEY AT THE TOP.

MAKE RAFT AS SHOWN ON FOLLOWING PAGE OR WITH STEEL BARRELS.

CLOTH COVERING CAN BE EITHER CANVAS OR OLD BED SHEETS.

SECTION A
OF SIDE & BOTTOM
PANELS.

APPROX
10"

16'

8'

8'

A

RAFT· MADE FROM
1X10 PLANKS & ¼"
MARINE PLYWOOD.

RIBS - MADE FROM
CURTAIN RODS OR
REINFORCING RODS·
(ASK YOUR LOCAL
BUILDING CONTRACTOR
FOR SPARES).

RODS

DETAIL
"B"

STITCH CLOTH
TOGETHER
OVER RIBS.

COVERING — MADE
FROM ANY AVAILABLE
CLOTH. OLD BED SHEETS
WILL DO, BUT CANVAS
IS BETTER.

CURTAIN ROD
BRACKET

DECORATIVE EYE.
PAINT BLACK &
WHITE

BRACKET
HOLDS RODS IN
PLACE YET ALLOWS
THEM TO TURN.

DETAIL "B"
(INSIDE VIEW)

WHALE RAFT (DETAILS) 39

DIVING BOARD

CABIN MADE FROM SPARE WOOD AND PANELING

NOTE:
SAME HULL AS SHOWN ON PREVIOUS PAGE.

OLD TIRES

TUG BOAT RAFT

IF YOU ARE GOING TO THE TROUBLE OF MAKING A RAFT, WHY NOT AN IMAGINATIVE ONE LIKE THIS "TUG BOAT RAFT". USE WHATEVER MATERIALS YOU HAVE OR CHANGE THE DESIGN TO SUIT YOUR CHILDREN.

MODEL SAIL BOAT

STRING

¼" TEMP. MASONITE

BALLOON

GLUE

CHEEK PLATE

CLOTH STRIPS
GLUED TO RUDDER
& KEEL

STEAM BOAT

THIS MODEL STEAM BOAT CAN BE MADE CHEAPLY AND EASILY WITH A FEW SMALL PIECES OF WOOD, WIRE, SCRAP METAL, AN OLD CAN, TUBING, AND A CAN OF STERNO.
THE BOAT IS PROPELLED BY STEAM MADE BY HEATING WATER IN A CAN AND FORCING THE STEAM THROUGH A TUBE OUT AT THE BACK.

COAT HANGER WIRE BENT & SOLDERED TO WOOD SCREW.

¾" WOOD CUT & SHAPED 10" LONG

METAL RUDDER SOLDERED TO WIRE.

SOLDER EDGE

METAL KEEL

OLD PAINT OR GLUE CAN

ENGINE

STERNO

¼" COPPER TUBING

STEAM

4 FT. SAIL-BOAT

H₂0

60"

COTTON SAIL

40"

10"

COAT V-SHAPED
GAP WITH GLUE AND
NAIL IN WEDGE-
SHAPED WOOD
STRIP

BRASS NAILS

30"

MAST

USE SCREW EYES
TO FASTEN BOOM
TO MAST

PIN TILLER TO
REAR DECK

NOTE:

USE MARINE
PLYWOOD THROUGHOUT!

6ft.

SAIL-BOAT

1½" × 8' SPRUCE MAST

1½" × 5' SPRUCE BOOM

HARDWOOD

BOW SUPPORT

KEEL

CENTERBOARD

MAST STEP

¼" MARINE PLYWOOD DECK

COCKPIT

¾" MARINE PLYWOOD TRANSOM

SPLASH BOARD

PULLEY

RUBBER OR PLASTIC HOSE EDGING.

72"

30"

½" MARINE PLYWOOD

¼" MARINE PLYWOOD

8"

5"

14"

CROSS SECTION OF CENTER BOARD

¼" ROUND

NOTCH OUT

½" MARINE PLYWOOD

GLUE & BOLT THROUGH

SPINE & CENTER-BOARD WELL-MADE FROM 3 CONTINUOUS PIECES OF MARINE PLYWOOD.

¼" ½" ¼"

MAST STEP

SQUARE OFF END OF MAST

KEEL

TILLER

PINTLE & GUDGEON BOUGHT AT MOST MARINE HARDWARE STORES

RUDDER

CROSS SECTION OF KEEL & SPINE.

6-FOOT SAILBOAT (DETAILS) 45

ROW-BOAT

STEP 2.
SOAK SIDE BOARDS IN WATER FOR SEVERAL DAYS AND BEND AROUND SPACER.

STEP 3.
FASTEN SIDE BOARDS SECURELY TO TRANSOM AND SAW OFF EXCESS.

STEP 1.
FASTEN BOW TOGETHER

STEP 4.
GLUE & SCREW FLOOR PANEL TO SIDE BOARDS & TRANSOM. AND TRIM OFF.

SPACER

2½'

6 FT.

3'

12"

HARDWOOD

SIDE PANEL

GLUE & SCREW

SECTION OF BOW ASSEMBLY

SUGGESTIONS

THE HOUSE FOR THE HOUSEBOAT
CAN BE MADE SEVERAL WAYS:
- ONE WAY IS TO MAKE IT OUT OF
3/4" PLYWOOD WITH A MINIMUM
AMOUNT OF FRAMING. (EASIEST)
- ANOTHER WAY IS TO ROUGH-FRAME
THE HOUSE WITH 2x4's AND COVER
WITH 1/8" MASONITE (TEMPERED) OR
1/4" PLYWOOD AND PAINT. (CHEAPEST)
- A THIRD WAY IS TO USE 2x2
FRAMING AND CLAP BOARD SIDING
WITH T&G ROOFING COVERED WITH
SHINGLES. (BEST BUT EXPENSIVE.)

HOUSE BOAT

CANVAS

CUT-AWAY
VIEW

LEAVE OPENINGS IN
DECK TO CHECK
FOR LEAKS.

8'X16' RAFT
MADE FROM 1X6
T&G & 1X12 CROSS
MEMBERS.
FIBERGLAS JOINTS AND
PAINT BOTTOM WITH POLYESTER RESIN.

INDOOR PROJECTS

INDOOR PROJECTS

DOLL HOUSE

WALLS & ROOF
MADE OF
1/8" MASONITE

DECORATE
WITH STRIPS
OF BALSA
WOOD

YELLOW
YARN

PAPER
SHINGLES

CLAY

SECTION
SWINGS
OUT

1/4" PLYWOOD
BASE

BALSA WOOD

PIÑATA PARTY

THE PIÑATA IS A MEXKAN TRADITION ORIGINALLY USED DURING THE NINE DAYS OF CHRISTMAS. IN PRESENT-DAY MEXICO THEY ARE USED AT BIRTHDAY PARTIES AND GENERALLY FILLED WITH FRUIT AND CANDY AND SOME-TIMES TOYS. THE PIÑATA IS HUNG FROM THE CEILING AND EACH CHILD IS GIVEN A CHANCE TO BREAK IT WITH A STICK. WHEN IT FINALLY DOES BREAK THERE IS A MAD SCRAMBLE FOR THE GOODIES INSIDE.

How To Make A Piñata

STEP 1. Blow up a balloon and wrap it with newspaper strips soaked in flour paste (papier-maché). After you have covered it with three or four layers allow to dry overnight.

NEWSPAPER STRIPS

FLOUR

BALLOON

WATER

BEAK & CROWN CUT OUT FROM CARDBOARD

NEWSPAPER CONE

FOLDED NEWSPAPER TAIL

STEP 2.
Deflate the balloon and paste on neck and tail made from old newspapers. Cut out beak and crown from cardboard and paste into slot cut in top of neck. Cut cross in bottom and insert presents wrapped in tissue paper. Close hole with newspapers and paste. Allow to dry.

HOLE

COLORED PAPER STRIPS CURLED AND PASTED TO TAIL

STEP 3.
Attach a loop of string at top to hang the piñata by. Paste on cardboard wings and paper frills on neck & tail. Cover with colored crépe paper.

RED

YELLOW

STRING

WHITE CRÉPE PAPER

ORANGE

CARDBOARD WINGS COVERED WITH CRÉPE PAPER

WIRE WRAPPED WITH ORANGE CRÉPE PAPER

Hints on Making Clay Structures

Use a good grade of water-base clay. Knead the clay on a piece of plaster so it is somewhat heavier than thick peanut-butter. Use the methods shown below for building up strong structures. Allow several days to dry. Structures may be painted with ordinary enamel paint or they may be fired in a kiln in sections.

Ways to Make Clay Stronger

1. Reinforce with ½" grid wire mesh.

2. Knead sand into clay

Kneading plate (made of plaster cast from baking tin.)

SAND

For moving parts, insert metal screw eyes while the clay is soft, secure with nail later.

Pinch Method

Always start with a very thick wall at bottom and work to a thin wall at top.

Build up structure by taking small flat pieces and pinching them over edge. Smooth with thumb.

You can make any structure you want if you follow these basic principles

WHEELBARROW

DOWEL

$\frac{3}{4}$" PLYWOOD

3 FT

ROOF LIFTS UP
FOR ACCESS.

WHEELBARROW HOUSE
IDEAL FOR PICKING UP TOYS

ROUND HOUSE
Toy Pick-up

DIXIE CUP

CARDBOARD TUBE

CORRUGATED CARDBOARD SHINGLES

SHINGLES MADE FROM CORRUGATED CARDBOARD - PAINT

1X2

NOTCH OUT

1/8" MASONITE

SCREW TO DOOR FRAME

HINGE

SCREW TO BOTTOM

HANDLE

2X2 SHAPED

3/4" PLYWOOD CIRCLE

4 CASTERS - BOLT TO BASE.

TOY BINS

FROG

SERVE AS STORAGE FOR SMALL TOYS AND MAKE PICKING UP TOYS FUN FOR THE CHILD.

BOLT & WASHER BECOME EYE OF FROG

MADE ENTIRELY FROM ½" PLYWOOD.

USE ⅛" HARDBOARD. SOAK IN HOT WATER FOR 1 HR. BEFORE BENDING.

FISH

½" PLYWOOD

PAINT DIFFERENT SHADES OF BLUE.

SOMETIMES NAILS COME IN ROUND BOXES LIKE THIS

LIFT OFF LID

TURTLE

KANGAROO

THE "KANGAROO" CAN SERVE AS A ROCKING TOY OR AS AN EXCELLENT PLACE TO STORE TOYS.

LEATHER EARS

HEAD MADE FROM THREE 2"x4"'S GLUED TOGETHER.

½" PLYWOOD

1 BOLT & WASHER

SEAT

¾" PLYWOOD LEGS

⅛" HARDBOARD

POUCH DOOR

EASY-TO-MAKE —

Llama

TOY PICK-UP

MADE FROM OLD 2 X 4's AND A BOX.

EARS MADE FROM LEATHER OR STIFF CLOTH.

TAIL MADE FROM OLD YARN

2'x4's

BOX

WHEEL ASSEMBLY

LAG SCREW

3 ROCKING HORSES

FELT

OLD WORK SOCK STUFFED WITH COTTON

2 X 4

OLD NAIL BARREL

OLD MOP

HERE ARE THREE ROCKING HORSES THAT CAN BE MADE IN LESS THAN A DAY AND WITH INEXPENSIVE MATERIALS. THE ONE ON THE LEFT IS MADE ENTIRELY FROM ARTICLES FOUND AROUND THE HOUSE.

1.

PLYWOOD ROCKING HORSE

2 X 4

¾" PLYWOOD

2.

ROCKING HORSE MADE FROM LOGS

DRILL ALL HOLES WITH EXPANSION BIT.

3.

EASY·TO·MAKE FURNITURE

IF YOU CAN'T FIND BIG PIECES OF WOOD YOU CAN TAKE SEVERAL 2×4'S, NAIL THEM TOGETHER AND TRIM THEM OFF WITH A PLANE. THIS TYPE OF FURNITURE IS QUICK AND EASY TO CONSTRUCT AND WILL LAST A LIFE-TIME.

WOODEN WEDGE

DRILL HOLE WITH EXPAN-ION BIT.

STAIN WALNUT

GLUE

PUNCH NAILS INTO WOOD & FILL HOLES.

DO MOST OF THE WORK WITH AN AXE. LEAVE FINISH ROUGH.

COST OF MATERIALS - $00.00

Two Rocking Chairs

MADE FROM BRANCHES

ROUND OFF EDGES WITH KNIFE

OR

3 LEGGED CHAIR

CLOTHES HANGER

Marble Ladder

PERFECT FOR A RAINY DAY !

THE MARBLE LADDER IS MADE FROM ANYTHING YOU CAN FIND. THE DESIGN YOU SEE HERE GIVES AN IDEA OF THE MANY THINGS YOU CAN USE. BUILD IT SO THAT WHEN THE MARBLE ROLLS DOWN IT MAKES AS MANY DIFFERENT SOUNDS AS POSSIBLE.

DROP MARBLE HERE

GROOVE

FUNNEL

CIGAR BOX WITH HOLES CUT IN BOTTOM

CARDBOARD CHANNEL BENT INTO CURVES.

BAFFLE MADE FROM STIFF PAPER ROLLED AROUND A NAIL.

SPOON WITH BALANCING WEIGHT

46 FLUORESCENT TUBE

BAKING PAN

COFFEE CAN

OUTDOOR PROJECTS

CROSS BOW

LEMON WOOD FLAT BOW

CROSS SECTION

TARGETS LIKE THESE CAN BE MADE TO FLOAT ON WATER. THE ARROWS WILL FLOAT, TOO.

WEIGHT

CARVED OR PAINTED DECORATION

STRING

ARROW

TRIGGER MECHANISM

CANNON

CLEAN-OUT PLUG

5"

JOINTING
COMPOUND

BELL

30"

COUPLINGS

BELL

BARREL OF CANNON MADE
FROM BITUMINIZED-FIBER
SEWER PIPE.

THIS CANNON IS A GOOD
TOY FOR ANY BOY FROM
SIX TO TWELVE. IT IS COM-
PLETELY HARMLESS AND
IS DESIGNED TO SHOOT
SOFT BALLS.

THE BARREL IS MADE
FROM PIECES OF SEWER
PIPE, ALL OF WHICH YOU
CAN FIND AT YOUR LOCAL
PLUMBING SUPPLIER OR
MAIL ORDER CATALOG FOR
ABOUT FIVE DOLLARS.

BASE MADE FROM 1"x6" BOARD.
REVERSE DIRECTION OF BOARD
FOR DOUBLE THICKNESS AND
NAIL TOGETHER.

LAG BOLTS

TO LOAD:
COMPRESS FIRING MECHANISM
WITH PLUNGER AND LOCK
TRIGGER IN PLACE.

PLUNGER - MADE
FROM CORK FISHERMAN
FLOATS.

RELEASE

STRING

SCREW EYE

SPRING

OAK

TRIGGER MECHANISM

STRIKE PLATE

FIRING MECHANISM

PAINT
BLACK

SOFTBALL

OLD MATTRESS SPRING

Horse

1" GALV. PIPES & JOINTS

NEWSPAPER

BURLAP

RAG MOP

COTTON MATTRESS STUFFING

½" WIRE MESH

PADDED CANVAS

HINGE

WAGON WHEEL

THIS HORSE CAN BE A LOT OF FUN FOR BOYS FROM THE AGE EIGHT TO TWELVE. ALTHOUGH THE HORSE STRUCTURE CAN BE MADE OF WOOD IT WILL LAST A LOT LONGER IF MADE WITH PIPE AS SHOWN AT LE

CARE SHOULD BE TAK TO PROVIDE A SOFT COVERING BELOW TH HORSE IN CASE THE RIDER SHOULD FALL. KEEP WHEELS WIDE AND LOW TO THE GROUND TO PREVENT HORSE FROM TIPPING OVER.

Pirate's Ship

BEGIN BY BUILDING THE BOTTOM FLOOR OUT OF 2×4's AND PLANKS.

SPREADER (TEMPORARY)

¾" THICK TRANSOM

¼" TEMPERED MASONITE 4'×8'

BOW STEM

2×4

BOTTOM FLOOR 2×4's & PLANKS

CUT OUT SIDE PANELS TO APPROXIMATE SHAPE AND NAIL THEM TO THE BOTTOM FLOOR. NAIL A SPREADER TEMPORARILY TO THE TOP TO BOW OUT THE SIDES, AND THEN FIT & NAIL THE BOW STEM & TRANSOM IN PLACE.

TRIM

MAST IS MADE FROM TWO PIECES OF 2×4 NAILED TOGETHER AND ROUNDED OFF AT THE EDGES.

BOTTOM OF MAST IS IMBEDDED IN GROUND.

BOW SPRIT

NAIL THE SIDE PANELS TO THE TOP FLOOR BOARDS. (THE SIDE PANEL SHOULD LAP OVER THE FLOOR SO THAT THE FLOOR SERVES AS A SPREADER AND THE SIDES AS SUPPORT.)

Pirate's Ship
CONSTRUCTION DETAILS

RAILING POSTS MADE FROM ¼" PLYWOOD OR MASONITE. USE CARDBOARD TEMPLATE. NAIL SEVERAL PIECES TOGETHER AND CUT OUT AT ONE TIME.

NAIL THRU

SABER SAW

JOLLY ROGER

CROW'S NEST MADE FROM SLATS OF WOOD AND TWO METAL STRAPS

ROPE LADDER

CARDBOARD TEMPLATE

2X4

RAILING DETAIL

PAINT BLACK & WHITE

BLUE BEARD

REAR VIEW

RUBBER STRAP FROM INNER TUBE

TENNIS BALL

MAILING TUBE BOUGHT AT STATIONERY STORE

CARRIAGE BOLTS

¾ PLYWOOD

CANNON

SHELF SCREWED TO INSIDE

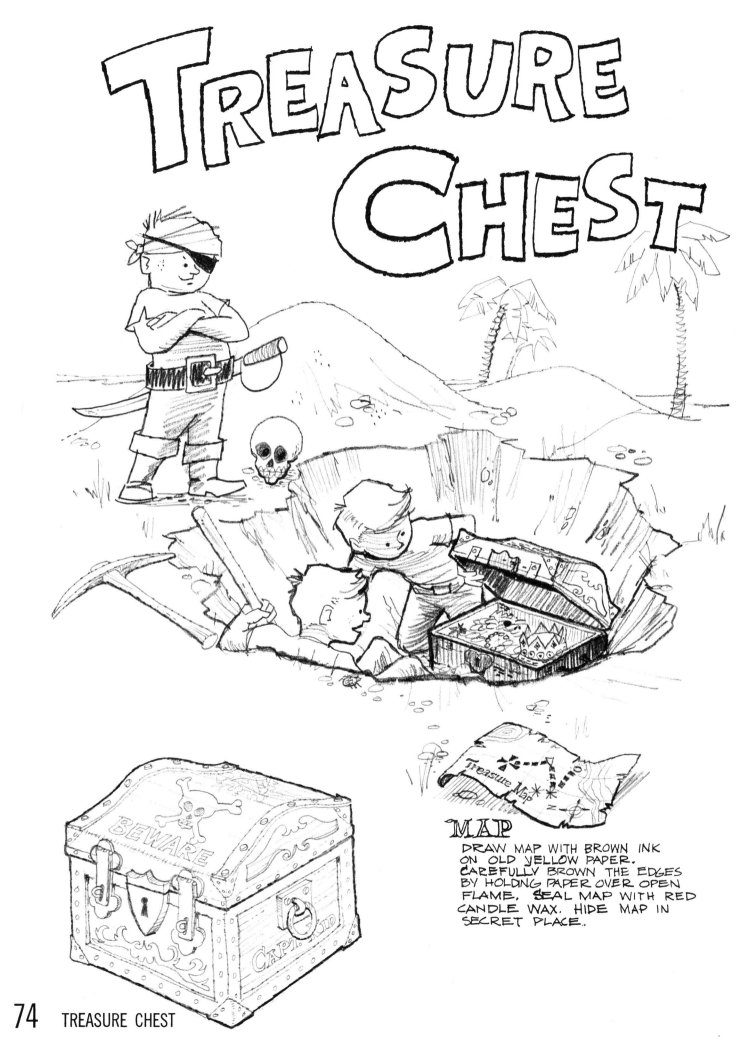

TREASURE CHEST

MAP

DRAW MAP WITH BROWN INK
ON OLD YELLOW PAPER.
CAREFULLY BROWN THE EDGES
BY HOLDING PAPER OVER OPEN
FLAME. SEAL MAP WITH RED
CANDLE WAX. HIDE MAP IN
SECRET PLACE.

¾" PLYWOOD, STAIN DARK WALNUT

OLD SHEET METAL PAINT BLACK

TRAP METAL LAG BOLTS PAINT GOLD

DECORATIVE TRAP HINGES PAINT GOLD

DECORATIVE ⅛" CUT OUT TEMPERED MASONITE PAINT GOLD

BRASS RIVETS

HANDLE MADE FROM IRON RING & "U" BOLT

¼" X 2" WOOD STRIPPING PAINT BLACK

REAR

BRASS CORNER BRACE CAN BE BOUGHT IN MOST LUGGAGE STORES

FAKE LOCK CUT OUT OF ¾" PLYWOOD AND PAINTED BLACK.

½" X 2" SLATS BEVEL EDGES WITH PLANE FOR PERFECT FIT

¼" X 2" WOOD STRIPPING WITH ½" OVERHANG HELPS SEAL CHEST, PAINT BLACK.

DECORATIVE CUTOUT WITH ½" OVERHANG

FRONT LOCKS

STANDARD LATCH & PAD-LOCK SCREWED INTO ⅛" MASON-ITE PLATE.

BRONCO

MADE FROM 24 FT. OF 2 X 6 BOARDS.

EARS MADE FROM OLD LEATHER

SEAT MADE FROM OLD BLANKET & ROPE.

OLD MOP HEAD

WHEELS MADE FROM 2 PIECES OF 2 X 6

HEAD PIVOTS UP & DOWN

BOLT THRU.

LEG DETAIL

SPRING RESTS IN HOLE

WOOD SPACER

¾" PIPE

DRILL ¾" HOLE THRU BOTTOM OF LEG TO HOLD SPRING.

COVERED WAGON

THE COVERED WAGON IS AN ANTIQUE AND IF CAREFULLY
CONSTRUCTED, SHOULD BE A SOURCE OF PRIDE FOR BOTH
FATHER & SON. MEASURES WERE TAKEN IN THIS DESIGN
TO SIMPLIFY CONSTRUCTION. SINCE THE WHEELS ARE
THE HARDEST PART TO MAKE, IF YOU CAN FIND ANY OLD
WAGON WHEELS IN A LOCAL ANTIQUE STORE, YOU WILL
SAVE YOURSELF A GREAT DEAL OF TIME.

8'

42"

18"

FOOTREST

BRAKE

HOOP BRACKETS

BOTTOM VIEW

WAGON TONGUE
(OPTIONAL)
SEE BELOW

FASTEN AXLE SECURELY
TO FRAME WITH BOLTS.

AXLE

DETAIL
SHOWING FRONT VIEW
OF WAGON TONGUE
CONNECTION

SPACER

ALLOW CLEARANCE
FOR PIVOTING

SPACERS

WEDGES

GLUE

12 SPOKES 1 X 2⅛

DRILL HOLE
AT EXACT CENTER
WITH EXPANSION BIT.

1⅝"

⅛" METAL STRAP

3-PLY ⅛" TEMP
MASONITE GLUED.

½" THICK
SPACER

SPOKE
MADE FROM 1 X 2's.

TO IMPROVE
APPEARANCE
ROUND OFF
SPOKES WITH
A SPOKE SHAVE
OR RASP AND
SAND SMOOTH.

6" DIA. PLYWOOD

WHEEL ASSEMBLY

MADE FROM
SPARE PIPE

AXLE
1¼" O.D. STEEL
PIPE.

SPOKE

CROSS SECTION

COTTER PIN

CAP

STEEL PIPE
SLEEVE FITS
INSIDE AXLE
PIPE.

SPOKE

BENT
CURTAIN
ROD

CANVAS

ROPE-
SEWN
IN HEM

GET A
Horse

Scooter

SCRAP WOOD

OLD SODA BOX

SCOOTERS LIKE THESE ARE MADE BY KIDS IN CITIES ALL OVER UNITED STATES.

OLD HINGES SERVE AS BRACKETS

ALTERNATE-STYLE SCOOTER MADE FROM OLD SODA BOX. HAS SPECIAL STORAGE COMPARTMENT.

TWO HALVES OF OLD ROLLER SKATE SCREWED TO BOTTOM OF 2X4.

FASTEN FRONT SKATE WITH ONE BOLT SO WHEELS CAN TURN SLIGHTLY

Wishing Well

NAILING STRIPS

ROUNDED WOOD
SHINGLES

¼" EXTERIOR
PLYWOOD

CUT ¼" NO
IN TOP O
PIPE

PIPE
INSERT

BALL
BEARING

CUT & BEND END
OF ALUMINUM PIPE TO
FIT TOP OF ROOF.

CUT FROM 2 X 8
WITH SABER SAW

USE OAK IF
AVAILABLE

START WITH
ROUND HOLE
AND CHISEL
OUT SQUARE

SQUARE
OFF END

WOODEN
SLATS

POURING
HANDLE

WHITE OAK

BOTTOM

DADO CUT

SIDE

METAL STRAP

DETAIL - CROSS
SECTION OF BUCKET

12 RAFTERS FASTENED TO HARDBOARD CIRCLE.

2 X 8 WOOD POSTS

CARRIAGE BOLTS.

MORTISE & TENON JOINT

NOTCH

3-PLY OF ⅛" TEMPERED HARDBOARD

STAGGER JOINTS

GLUE

CUT RAFTERS FROM BOARD 4'X1"X 8' WITH SABER SAW.

STONE

STEPS

DRAIN

HIDDEN VALVE BOX.

WATER SUPPLY LINE

"THICK CONC. BASE

GRAVEL & LOOSE STONE

SLANT PIPE BACK TO WATER SUPPLY AND PROVIDE DRAIN-OFF.

WISHING WELL (DETAILS) 83

Jungle Drum

$1\frac{1}{2}"$

LEAVE ONE END CLOSE

SAW LOG IN HALF

FILL SCREW HOLE WITH DOWELS

GLUE & SCREW

FIND A BIG LOG - AS THICK AS POSSIBLE - AND SAW IT OFF AT 3 TO 4 FT. STRIP OFF THE BARK AND SAW IT IN HALF. HOLLOW OUT EACH HALF WITH A CHISEL AND JOIN THEM TOGETHER WITH GLUE AND SCREWS. SUSPEND DRUM FROM TREE WITH TWO ROPES.

Witch Doctor

TIGER-TOOTH NECKLACE

PLASTER TEETH MADE FROM LATEX MOLD, SHELLACKED

VOO DOO MASK

WOOD DOWEL

DRIED GOURD

RATTLE

HORSE-HAIR OR MOP HEAD

CHICKEN WIRE

LEATHER SHOULDER STRAPS

PAPIER MACHE OVER WIRE

DART

PAPER

CORK

BLOW-GUN

CLEAT

RAILROAD ENGINE

A RAILROAD ENGINE LIKE THIS IS NOT AS HARD TO MAKE AS IT MIGHT APPEAR. THE FRONT-END CYLINDER IS A PAPER PACKING BARREL. THE SMOKE STACK IS MADE FROM AN OLD WASTE PAPER BASKET AND A LAMP SHADE. TAKE THE WHEELS FROM OLD BICYCLES, TRICYCLES OR BABY CARRIAGES. ADD A MASONITE OR PLYWOOD COVER PLATE OVER THE WHEELS AND PAINT ON BLACK SPOKES. IF DESIRED THE ENGINE CAN BE RUN ON A TRACK OVER A PREDETERMINED COURSE (A SECTION OF THE TRACK IS SHOWN AT THE BOTTOM OF THE NEXT PAGE.)

OLD LAMPSHADE

OLD POT WITH HANDLE CUT OFF.

OLD WASTE-PAPER BASKET

PACKING BARREL

TIN CAN

¼" TEMP MAS-ONITE, BENT & SCREWED TO FRAME.

CAB

(PAINT FLAT BLACK WITH GOLD TRIM.)

BICYCLE WHEEL & COASTER BRAKE.

¼" PLYWOOD COVER

FRAME

1 x 2

COWCATCHER

WHEELS FROM OLD BABY CARRIAGE OR TRICYCLE.

PISTON ROD PIVOTS ON WHEEL.

THIS END RESTS IN SLOT IN PISTON BOX.

PISTON BOX

TRACK (OPTIONAL)

¼ ROUND MOLDING

2 x 4

CROSS SECTION

MADE COMPLETLY FROM MATERIALS FOUND AROUND THE HOUSE..

RAILROAD ENGINE (DETAILS) 87

JokeBox

THIS INNOCENT LOOKING BOX HOLDS A SURPRISE FOR ANY CURIOUS PERSON OPENING IT. WRITTEN ON THE OUTSIDE ARE THE WORDS "WORLD'S MOST DANGEROUS ANIMAL". WHEN OPENED, THE BOX REVEALS A DARK CAGE WITH GRASS IN IT. ON CLOSER INSPECTION THE OBSERVER SEES HIMSELF REFLECTED IN A MIRROR.

1X6

1X4

MIRROR GLUED TO BACK WALL

GRASS

$\frac{1}{2}$" WIRE MESH

1X6 DOOR

WORLD'S MOST DANGEROUS ANIMAL

ONCE THE JOKE HAS RUN IT'S COURSE, THE BOX CAN BE USED AS A MAIL BOX OR A PLACE TO LEAVE MESSAGES.

PAD & PENCIL

MAIL

Scooter
from a
SkateBoard

An old skateboard can be converted into a terrific scooter by adding just a few pieces of wood.

PLAN VIEW
16"
HANDLE

1"
7"
TOP
4"
4½"
1¼" SCREWS

3½"
1×6
3"
5½"
66°

24"

SHELF
¾" PLY.

¾" PLY.
BASE
3½"

3"
6"

BASE

¾"×1½"
BOLT

¾" PLY.

TANK

PAINT OLIVE DRAB

FOLD-AWAY SEAT

TRAP DOOR

FRAME WITH 1x2'S AND COVER WITH PLANKS

A TANK LIKE THIS CAN PROVIDE ENDLESS FUN FOR ALL THE KIDS, IN SUMMER AND WINTER. IT FEATURES A REVOLVING TURRET AND A CANNON THAT SHOOTS WATER AT THE ENEMY. YOU CAN MOVE IT WITHOUT EX- POSING YOURSELF TO THE ENEMY BY OPENING A TRAP DOOR IN THE BOTTOM AND PUSHING THE TANK FROM THE INSIDE.

PLASTIC SEWER PIPE

PEEP HOLE

COVER

BICYCLE PUMP
MAKES AN EXCELLENT
WATER GUN.

GOLF BALL ACTS
AS BALL BEARING

GUIDE

GLUE
& SCREW

THREE LAYERS OF ¼" MASONITE
BENT INTO CIRCLE.

TURRET

ALTHOUGH THIS PROJECT
MAY REQUIRE A LITTLE
MONEY AND A LOT OF TIME,
YOU WILL FIND THE END
RESULT WELL WORTH IT.

SEAT

COVER

TOP VIEW

PIN

2×4

PIPE

PIPE
CAP

WOOD
DOWEL
PLUG

WHEEL DETAIL

2 PIECES OF
2×12 SCREWED
TOGETHER

FRAMING & CONSTRUCTION DETAILS.

48"

DOUBLE-THICK FLOORS

18"

PLAN LAYOUT OF 2"x4" STUD SUPPORTS

2×4's   2×4's

60"

24" OPENING

DOOR →

⅛" TEMPERED MASONITE

COVER TOP WITH SHEET METAL

DOOR

SCREW FROM INSIDE

2" DIA. POLE SCREWED TO FIN.

U.S.

¾" PLYWOOD

FIN

28"

NOSE CONE

AIRPLANE

NOSE MADE FROM OLD PAIL.

WINDSHIELD MADE FROM CURTAIN RODS.

TAIL & WINGS MADE FROM ½" PLYWOOD

SLANT THIS PANEL BACK TO TRAILING EDGE OF TAIL.

SIMPLE BOX ½" PLYWOOD

1 X 2 STRUT

PROP SHAPED FROM 2 X 4

LEMONADE STAND

Lemonade 3¢

CANVAS ROOF
SUPPORTED BY RODS

PLASTIC TUBE

CASH BOX – MONEY
DROPS THRU SLOTS
INTO DRAWER.

1¢   5¢   10¢

DRAWER

CUPS

NOTCH
(CROSS SECTION)

2×2

VALVE

TOP VIEW

Traveling Zoo

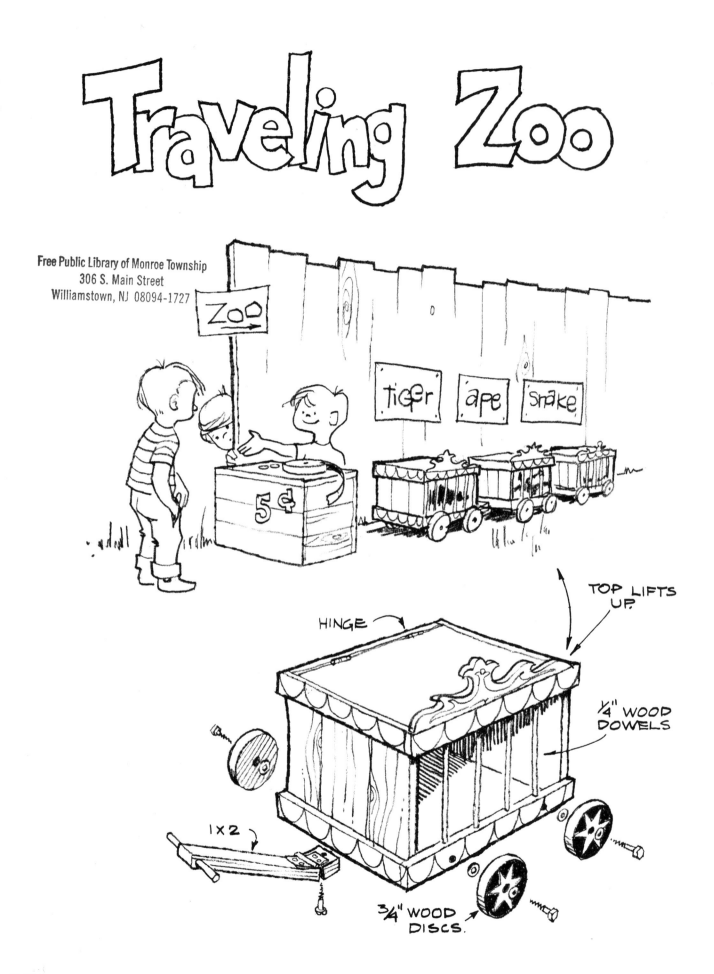

Zoo

tiger ape snake

5¢

TOP LIFTS UP.

HINGE

¼" WOOD DOWELS

1 X 2

¾" WOOD DISCS.